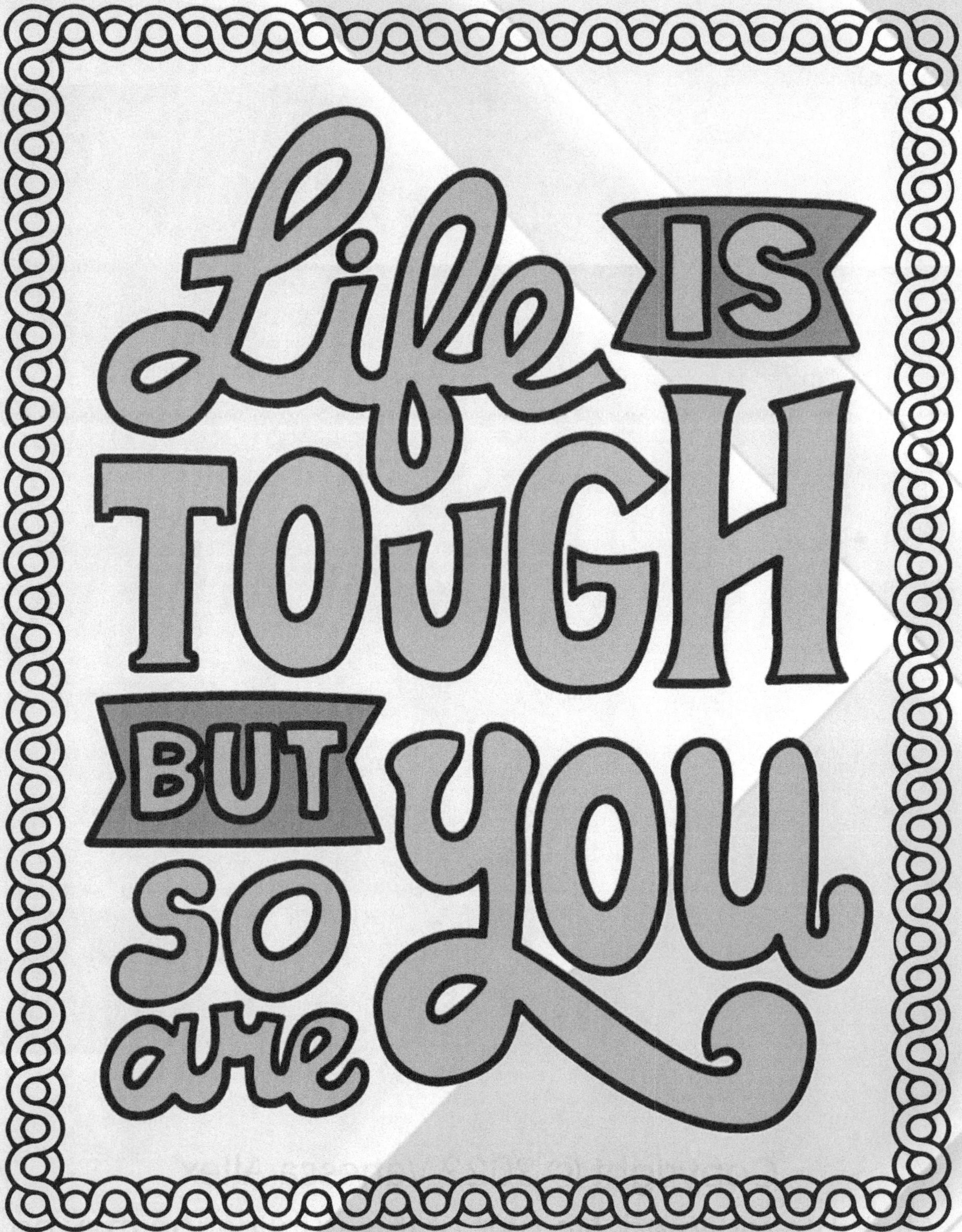
Life
IS
TOUGH
BUT
SO
are
YOU

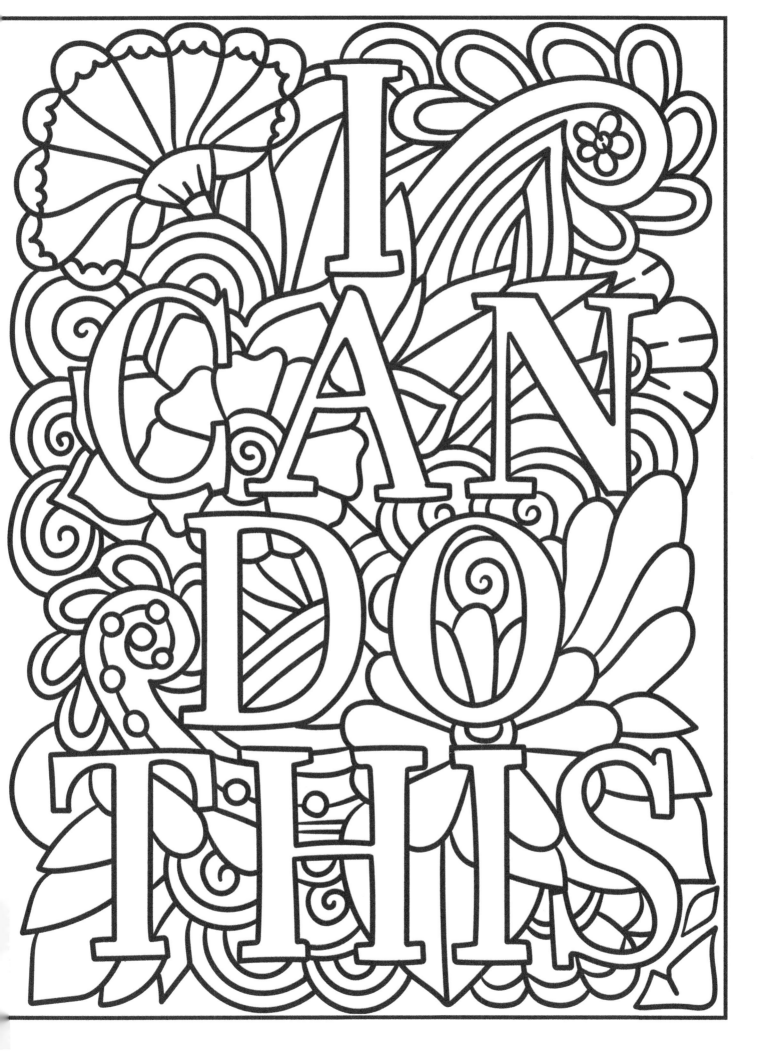

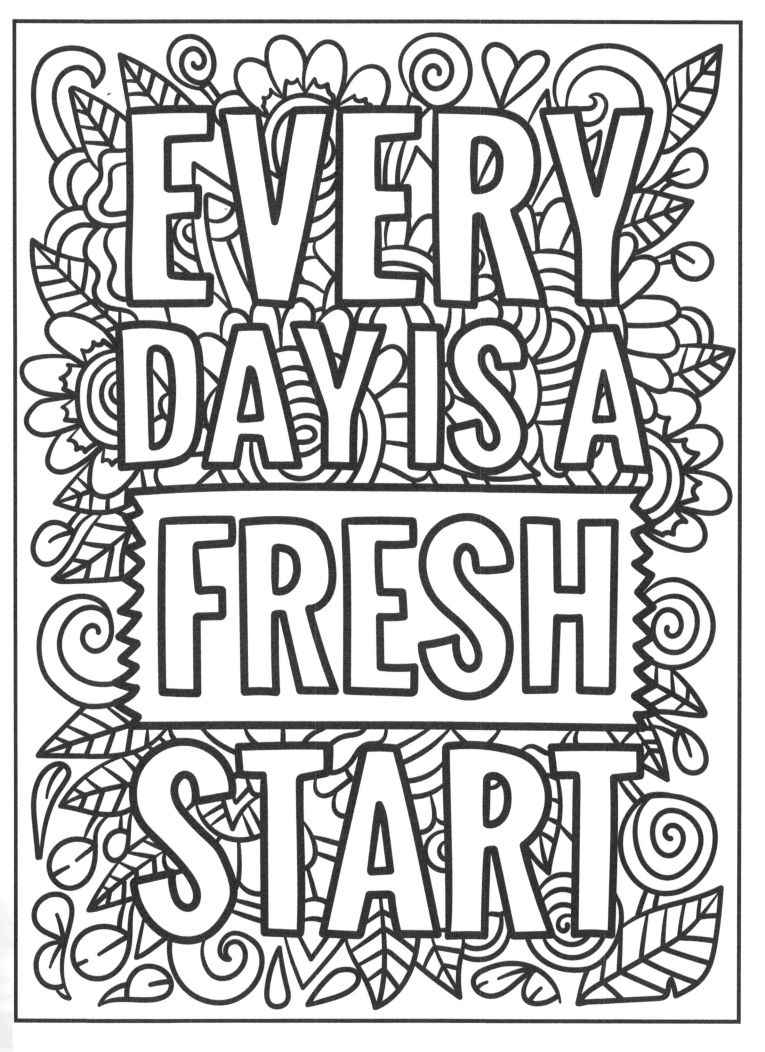

Use this page to test your crayons, pencils and felt tips to see what the color looks like on this paper.

Use this page to test your crayons, pencils and felt tips to see what the color looks like on this paper.

Use this page to test your crayons, pencils and felt tips to see what the color looks like on this paper.

Thank you...

...for purchasing this coloring book.

This book has been made especially for adults who enjoy easy coloring.
30 positive, inspirational, heart warming quotes to remind you, you've got this!

If this book met your expectations, please consider leaving a review from were you purchased it.

Thank you again.

Vanessa Allex

Made in the USA
Las Vegas, NV
20 August 2023

76305227R00039